United States Regions

Midwest and Great Lakes Regions

Nancy Allen

Educational Media

rourkeeducationalmedia.com

Scan for Related Titles and Teacher Resources

Before Reading:

Building Academic Vocabulary and Background Knowledge

Before reading a book, it is important to tap into what your child or students already know about the topic. This will help them develop their vocabulary, increase their reading comprehension, and make connections across the curriculum.

1. Look at the cover of the book. What will this book be about?
2. What do you already know about the topic?
3. Let's study the Table of Contents. What will you learn about in the book's chapters?
4. What would you like to learn about this topic? Do you think you might learn about it from this book? Why or why not?
5. Use a reading journal to write about your knowledge of this topic. Record what you already know about the topic and what you hope to learn about the topic.
6. Read the book.
7. In your reading journal, record what you learned about the topic and your response to the book.
8. After reading the book complete the activities below.

Content Area Vocabulary
Read the list. What do these words mean?

border
canals
commercial
economy
endangered species
habitats
manufacturing
migrate
nation
pollution
settlers
valleys

After Reading:

Comprehension and Extension Activity

After reading the book, work on the following questions with your child or students in order to check their level of reading comprehension and content mastery.

1. How were the Great Lakes formed? (Summarize)
2. What is the importance of Chicago for businesses across the country? (Infer)
3. Why are the Great Lakes important in manufacturing goods? (Asking questions)
4. What is the major crop of the Midwest? Why? (Summarize)
5. What are activities you'd like to do on the Great Lakes? (Text to Self Connection)

Extension Activity

The Midwest farmers produce much of the corn in our country. Why do we need so much corn? How much corn do you actually consume? Look at the labels of various food products in your home such as cereal, bread products, pasta, or other boxed items. What are the ingredients? How much is corn based? What other types of products contain corn?

Table of Contents

The Midwest and Great Lakes

The Midwest region is called the heartland of America. The region got the name because it is in the center, or heart, of the United States.

The Midwest is located between the Appalachian Mountains and the Rocky Mountains. The Ohio River borders on the south. Canada borders on the north.

States that fall in the Midwest region are Ohio, Indiana, Illinois, Missouri, Iowa, Minnesota, Wisconsin, and Michigan. Parts of Kansas and Nebraska are considered part of the Midwest as well.

Iowa Farm

Lake Huron

The Midwest and Great Lakes regions have farmland, lakes, coasts, and forests.

Sleeping Bear Beach, Michigan

Black Bear in Northern Michigan

The Great Lakes region borders the Midwest. The five Great Lakes are Superior, Michigan, Huron, Erie, and Ontario. Lake Michigan is the only Great Lake that is entirely in the U.S. The other four Great Lakes share a **border** with Canada. Rivers and **canals** connect the lakes to the Atlantic Ocean and the Gulf of Mexico.

Lake Ontario Toronto, Canada

The Great Lakes form the world's largest body of fresh water. The U.S. and Canada work together to care for these lakes. Both countries have passed clean water laws. The laws protect the lakes from **pollution**. The Great Lakes provide drinking water for many people. The laws also protect animals and their habitats.

	Lake Superior	Lake Michigan	Lake Huron	Lake Erie	Lake Ontario
Surface Area	31,700 square miles (82,000 square kilometers)	22,300 square miles (58,000 square kilometers)	23,000 square miles (60,000 square kilometers)	9,910 square miles (25,700 square kilometers)	7,340 square miles (19,000 square kilometers)
Water Volume	2,900 cubic miles (12,000 cubic kilometers)	1,180 cubic miles (4,900 cubic kilometers)	850 cubic miles (3,500 cubic kilometers)	116 cubic miles (480 cubic kilometers)	393 cubic miles (1,640 cubic kilometers)

Lake Superior is the largest of the Great Lakes. Next in size are Michigan and Huron. Lake Erie contains the least amount of water, and Lake Ontario has the smallest area.

The History of the Midwest and Great Lakes Regions

Sheets of ice, called glaciers, moved across the Midwest thousands of years ago. Glaciers carved hills, **valleys**, and large holes. The ice left much of the land flat. When the climate became warmer, the glaciers slowly melted. Melted glacier water filled the large holes and formed the Great Lakes.

For thousands of years, Native Americans lived in the Midwest. They lived off the land with its large supply of fish, game, and plants. In the 1800s, **settlers** moved to the Midwest in search of farmland. They found the rich soil was good for farming.

The region is called the nation's breadbasket because farmers grow wheat, oats, and corn. Bread is made from these grains.

Some of the people who settled the breadbasket came from the East and South. Many came from Europe. Most were looking for jobs in farming, mining, and manufacturing.

Muddy Trail Mix Recipe

Use crunch wheat cereal to make this Midwest treat.

Ingredients:

1 cup chocolate chips

1 stick butter

$\frac{1}{2}$ cup peanut butter

6 cups wheat squares cereal

1 cup raisins

1 cup walnuts or pecans

2 cups powdered sugar

Directions:

Melt chocolate chips, butter, and peanut butter in a microwave for about $1\frac{1}{2}$ minutes. Stir the mixture. Place the cereal in a large bowl. Pour the mixture over the cereal. Mix well. Pour powdered sugar, cereal mixture, raisins, and nuts into a large paper bag. Shake well until all pieces are coated. Pour the mixture onto a large cookie sheet to cool. Store Muddy Trail Mix in a sealed container.

Battle Creek, Michigan, is called the Cereal Capital of the World. The Kellogg brothers made the first dry cereal there in 1906. The cereal was Corn Flakes.

Americans eat about 160 bowls of cereal each year. One bushel of wheat will make 53 boxes of cereal.

Farming and Manufacturing

The Midwest and Great Lakes regions have many farms. The flat land and rich soil make for some of the best farmland in the U.S.

The long summers in Ohio, Indiana, Illinois, Iowa, and Missouri are perfect for growing corn. Corn is valuable to our nation's food supply because it is used in so many products.

The short summers in Minnesota, Michigan, and Wisconsin are better for growing grasses. The grass is fed to cattle that produce milk made into cheese and other dairy products.

Corn syrup is used to make ice cream and soft drinks. Flour is ground from corn and made into breads and pasta.

Corn is America's biggest crop. People around the world use corn for food.

Minnesota, Michigan, and Wisconsin have large forests. Pine, spruce, aspen, birch, oak, and maple trees are common. Wildflowers and grasses grow there, too. These plants provide food and **habitats** for animals. Moose, black bears, lynx, and wolves call these woods home.

The forests in the Great Lakes region are populated with owls, squirrels, and deer. The Great Lakes provide food for birds, such as the American Bittern, the Great Blue Heron, and the Wood Thrush.

The lakes are also used as a rest stop for Canada geese and other birds that **migrate.** These birds move from one place to another as the seasons change.

Canada Goose

Lake Michigan

*The Michigan monkey flower grows along the shore of Lake Michigan. The plant grows in cold, flowing water. It is an **endangered species**.*

Assembly lines, such as this one, are the common method of assembling complex items such as automobiles.

The Great Lakes are important to the region's **economy**. The lake waters are commonly used for **commercial** fishing.

In addition, **manufacturing** is big business in the Great Lakes region. Forest timber is used to make furniture, paper, and build homes. Iron is mined and made into steel. Coal is also mined and used to create electricity. Factories make machinery, automobiles, food, and tires.

With so many goods manufactured in the region, shipping is also important to the area's economy. The Great Lakes and the Mississippi, Missouri, and Ohio Rivers are major shipping routes that carry goods to be sold elsewhere.

Cuyahoga River, Cleveland, Ohio

The Mississippi River starts in Minnesota. The river forms a border for parts of Wisconsin, Iowa, Illinois, and Missouri.

Things to See and Do

Each year millions of people travel to the regions. They see steep hills and rolling plains, dense forests with sparkling waterfalls, and lots of lakes, large and small.

In winter, ice fishing is popular. Some visit to ski and ride snowmobiles. Others like dogsledding.

In summer, people enjoy the lakes in other ways. Boating, sailing, waterskiing, and fishing are popular sports. Hikers and bikers can enjoy thousands of miles of trails.

Diving among shipwrecks is popular with tourists. Storms on Lake Superior have sunk more than 300 ships.

In the Midwest, severe weather is common. When cool air from the north often meets warm air from the south, blizzards, thunderstorms, and tornadoes form quickly. Temperatures can swing above 100° Fahrenheit (38° Celsius) in summer. In winter, it can dip below 0° Fahrenheit (−17° Celsius). Rain often falls a few days a week from spring through autumn.

Minnesota is known as the Land of 10,000 Lakes. Some estimates put the number of lakes in Minnesota as high as 22,000.

The Midwest and Great Lakes regions are home to many cities. Chicago is the third largest city in the U.S. It is located in Illinois on Lake Michigan. Chicago is a transportation center for the whole country. Chicago's railroads handle more freight than any other city in the **nation**.

Detroit is known as Music City because of its jazz and blues music. Shipping is important to this city, too. Large ships, called freighters, travel to Detroit from more than 100 world ports. Freighters carry manufactured goods.

Detroit is also known as Motor City. In 1908, Henry Ford built the Model T. Many people bought the car due to its low cost. The auto industry soon became very important to Detroit's economy.

The Gateway Arch in Saint Louis, Missouri, is the tallest U.S. monument.

The Cincinnati Reds baseball team won two World Series. Chicago has two professional baseball teams. They are the Cubs and the White Sox.

The Midwest and Great Lakes regions are home to many sports teams and spectator sports. The Indianapolis 500 is a famous car race run annually in Indiana.

High school, college, and professional sports draw large crowds. Football, basketball, baseball, and soccer are also popular. Long winters and frozen ponds have made ice hockey a sport enjoyed by those who like to be outside in the cold.

Wrigley Field baseball stadium in Illinois is named for the same Wrigley that created Wrigley's chewing gum.

The Heartland Today

Today, the heartland of America offers something for everyone. If you like large cities, St. Louis has a storytelling festival. Cleveland has the largest indoor Ferris wheel.

If you like small towns, the heartland has those, too. The people are friendly and welcome tourists.

If a farm visit is your idea of fun, try finding your way through a cornfield maze. Maybe you would rather ride on a hay wagon or pick apples.

The Midwest and Great Lakes regions offer many reasons to live there or visit. The people and the heartland help make the United States a great country.

Johnny Appleseed planted apple trees in the Midwest. He wanted settlers who moved west to always have food to eat.

Pointe Betsie Lighthouse, Lake Michigan

Michigan is the only state that touches four of the five Great Lakes. Anywhere you travel in Michigan, you are within 85 miles (137 kilometers) of a Great Lake.

State Facts Sheet

Iowa

Motto: Our Liberties We Prize and Our Rights We will Maintain.

Nickname: Hawkeye State

Capital: Des Moines

Known for: Corn, Farms, and Rich Soil

Fun Fact: Wright County, Iowa has the highest percentage of grade-A topsoil in the U.S.

Minnesota

Motto: The Star of the North.

Nickname: Land of 10,000 Lakes

Capital: Saint Paul

Known for: Lakes, Corn, Cereal, and Dairy Products

Fun Fact: Minnesota has 90,000 miles (145,000 kilometers) of shores.

Wisconsin

Motto: Forward.

Nickname: Badger State and America's Dairyland

Capital: Madison

Known for: Cheese, Dairy Products, Lakes, and Fishing

Fun Fact: Wisconsin produces more cranberries than any other state and is home to the first kindergarten in the U.S.

Michigan

Motto: If You Seek a Pleasant Peninsula, Look About You.

Nickname: Wolverine State

Capital: Lansing

Known for: Great Lakes, Cherries, Farmland, and Automobile Manufacturing

Fun Fact: The lower part of the state, called Lower Michigan, is shaped like a mitten.

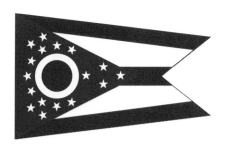

Ohio
Motto: With God, All Things Are Possible.

Nickname: Buckeye State

Capital: Columbus

Known for: Rich Soil, Factories, and
Birthplace of 8 U.S. Presidents

Fun Fact: Native Americans left over 6,000
burial mounds in the state.

Indiana
Motto: Crossroads of America.

Nickname: Hoosier State

Capital: Indianapolis

Known for: Farmland, Corn, Wildflowers,
and Racing

Fun Fact: Almost half the farmland in Indiana
is planted in corn.

Illinois
Motto: State Sovereignty, National Union.

Nickname: Land of Lincoln

Capital: Springfield

Known for: Lakes, Farming, Manufacturing,
and Native American Burial Grounds

Fun Fact: The world's first skyscraper was built
in Chicago, Illinois in 1885.

Missouri
Motto: The Welfare of the People Shall Be the
Supreme Law.

Nickname: Show Me State

Capital: Jefferson City

Known for: Farming, Corn, Wheat, Dairy, Timber,
and Cotton

Fun Fact: The first ice cream cones were made in
Saint Louis, Missouri in 1904.

State Facts Sheet

Think of HOMES
to remember the
Great Lakes: Huron,
Ontario, Michigan,
Erie, and Superior.

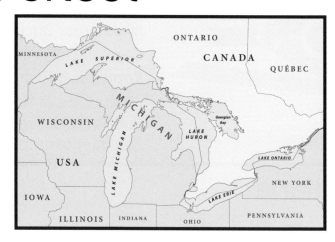

Lake Superior

- Largest freshwater lake in the world
- Coldest and deepest of the Great Lakes
- Deepest point is 1,333 feet (406 meters)
- Over 300 rivers and streams empty into the lake

Lake Michigan

- Deepest point is 925 feet (282 meters)
- Water temperature is 60–70° Fahrenheit (15–21° Celsius) in summer
- Grasses and sand dunes provide habitats for wildlife
- Trout, salmon, walleye, and smallmouth bass live in the lake

Lake Huron

- Named for the Wyandot Indians, or Hurons
- Longest shoreline of the Great Lakes
- Over 1,000 shipwrecks on the lake
- Water temperature reaches 73° Fahrenheit (23° Celsius) in summer
- 7,000-year-old petrified trees are underwater

Lake Erie

- Named for the Erie Native American tribe
- Water temperatures reach 70° Fahrenheit (21° Celsius) and above in summer
- Deepest point is 210 feet (64 meters)
- Water flows from Lake Erie to Niagara Falls

Lake Ontario

- Ontario is the Native American word meaning "shining water"
- Apple, pear, cherry, and plum orchards grow near the lake
- Deepest point is 801 feet (244 meters)
- The land bordering Lake Ontario gets up to 20 feet (6 meters) of snow each year

Glossary

border (BOR-dur): dividing line between two countries

canals (kuh-NALZ): waterways that are dug across land so that boats can travel between two bodies of water

commercial (kuh-MUR-shuhl): having to do with buying and selling

economy (i-KAH-nuh-mee): the system of buying, selling, making things, and managing money in a place

endangered species (en-DAYN-jured SPEE-sheez): a plant or animal that is in danger of disappearing forever

habitats (HAB-i-tats): places where an animal or plant is usually found

manufacturing (man-yuh-FAK-chur-ing): to make something

migrate (MYE-grate): to move from one area to another

nation (NAY-shuhn): a country

pollution (puh-LOO-shuhn): the action of making the land, water, and air not safe to use

settlers (SET-lerz): people who move to a new place to live

valleys (VAL-eez): low areas of land between two hills or mountains

Index

Show What You Know

1. Why did settlers move to the Midwest region?
2. What types of jobs can be found in the Midwest and Great Lakes regions?
3. Why do so many people visit these regions?
4. What are some popular sports in these regions?
5. How did the Midwest get its name?

Websites to Visit

www.sheppardsoftware.com/web_games.htm

www.kidskonnect.com/subjectindex/28-places/geography/
    415-great-lakes.html

hwww.wartgames.com/themes/50states/usregions.html

Author

Nancy Kelly Allen lives in Kentucky with her husband and two canine writing assistants, Jazi and Roxi. When Nancy leaves Kentucky, she often travels to the Midwest. She and her husband visit family in Ohio and buy apples. Each time she eats an apple, she thanks Johnny Appleseed for planting all those trees.

Meet The Author!
www.meetREMauthors.com

PHOTO CREDITS: Cover: ©JerryB7 (top left), ©emholk (top center), ©Xavier Arnau (top right), ©Andrew N Dierks (bottom left), ©RudyBalasko (bottom right); title page: ©Maksymowicz; page 3: ©Elenathewise; page 5: ©MaxyM (top left), ©John McCormick (top right), © maomejia (bottom left), ©Critterbiz (bottom right); page 6: ©SurangaSL; page 8: ©grafvision; page 9: ©Georgios Kolidas; page 11: ©Blend Images; page 12: ©M. Unal Ozmen; page 13: ©George Clerk; page 14: ©Yan Ke; page 15: ©doubleus; page 16: ©Rainer Plendl; page 17: ©StonePhotos; page 18: ©andyheiser; page 19: ©George Burba; page 20: ©dvmsimages; page 21: ©Rudy Balasko; page 22: ©Richard Paul Kane; page 23: ©Ffooter (top), ©Roman Samokhin (bottom); page 24: ©Mazzur; page 25: ©John McCormick; page 26, 27: ©Turovsky; page 28: ©fstockfoto (middle), ©Wolgin (bottom); page 29: ©ehrlif (top), ©Galyna Andrushko (middle), ©Marykit (bottom)

Edited by: Jill Sherman

Cover design by: Tara Raymo
Interior design by: Rhea Magaro

Library of Congress PCN Data

Midwest and Great Lakes Regions / Nancy Allen
(United States Regions)
 ISBN 978-1-62717-671-2 (hard cover)
 ISBN 978-1-62717-793-1 (soft cover)
 ISBN 978-1-62717-910-2 (e-Book)
Library of Congress Control Number: 2014934379

Also Available as:

Printed in the United States of America, North Mankato, Minnesota